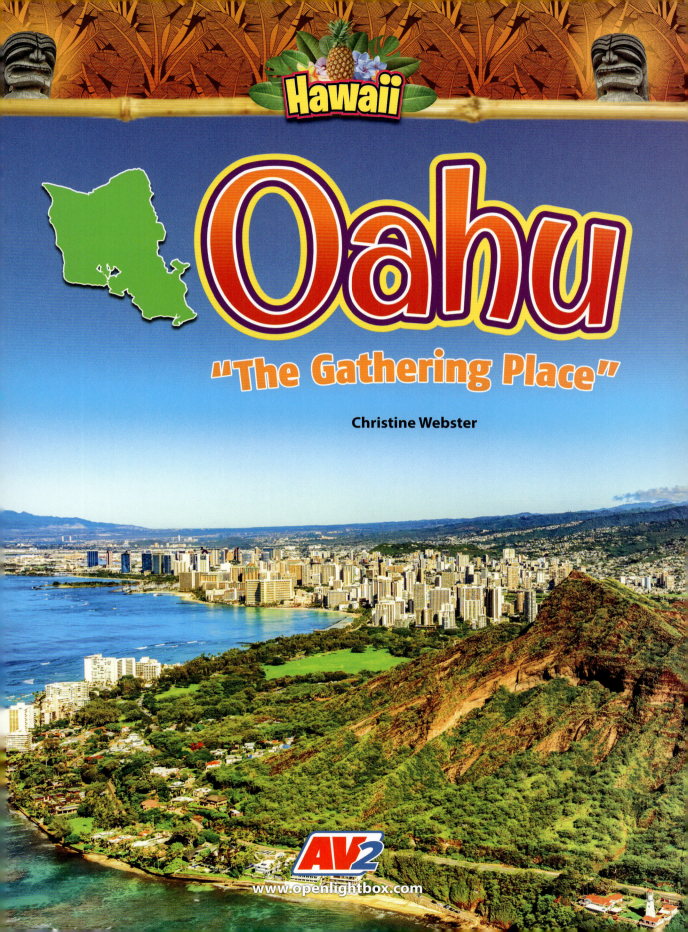
Hawaii
Oahu
"The Gathering Place"
Christine Webster

Step 1
Go to www.openlightbox.com

Step 2
Enter this unique code

VSQDY8AGS

Step 3
Explore your interactive eBook!

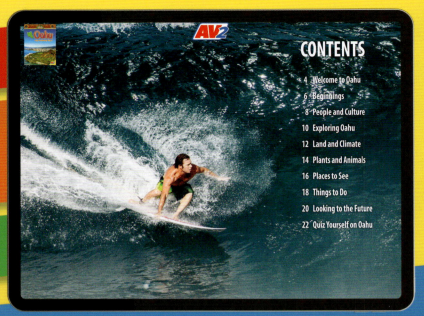

CONTENTS
- 4 Welcome to Oahu
- 6 Beginnings
- 8 People and Culture
- 10 Exploring Oahu
- 12 Land and Climate
- 14 Plants and Animals
- 16 Places to See
- 18 Things to Do
- 20 Looking to the Future
- 22 Quiz Yourself on Oahu

AV2 is optimized for use on any device

Your interactive eBook comes with...

 Contents Browse a live contents page to easily navigate through resources

 Audio Listen to sections of the book read aloud

 Videos Watch informative video clips

 Weblinks Gain additional information for research

 **Slideshows** View images and captions

 Try This! Complete activities and hands-on experiments

 Key Words Study vocabulary, and complete a matching word activity

 Quizzes Test your knowledge

 Share Share titles within your Learning Management System (LMS) or Library Circulation System

 Citation Create bibliographical references following APA, CMOS, and MLA styles

This title is part of our AV2 digital subscription

1-Year Grades K–5 Subscription
ISBN 978-1-7911-3320-7

Access hundreds of AV2 titles with our digital subscription.
Sign up for a FREE trial at www.openlightbox.com/trial

The digital components of this book are guaranteed to stay active for at least five years from the date of publication.

Hawaii

Oahu

"The Gathering Place"

CONTENTS
- 2 Interactive eBook Code
- 4 Welcome to Oahu
- 6 Beginnings
- 8 People and Culture
- 10 Exploring Oahu
- 12 Land and Climate
- 14 Plants and Animals
- 16 Places to See
- 18 Things to Do
- 20 Looking to the Future
- 22 Quiz Yourself on Oahu
- 23 Key Words/Index

OAHU—The Gathering Place 3

WELCOME TO Oahu

- Oahu is the **third-largest** Hawaiian Island, after Hawaii and Maui.
- Oahu is **44 miles** (71 kilometers) by **30 miles** (48 km) wide.
- Approximately **75 percent** of Hawaii's population lives on Oahu.

Aloha! Welcome to Oahu! Oahu is part of the Hawaiian Islands. This **archipelago** is made up of more than 130 islands that stretch across 1,500 miles (2,410 km) of the Pacific Ocean. Together, the Hawaiian Islands form the U.S. state of Hawaii, which became the 50th state in 1959.

As the most populated Hawaiian Island, Oahu is also known as "The Gathering Place." Hawaii's largest city and state capital, Honolulu, is found here. As a result, Oahu has become a place where people gather for business and tourism.

THE ISLAND OF Oahu

Population: 953,000 (2024)

Area: 597 square miles (1,546 sq. km)

Altitude: 4,025 feet (1,227 meters) at its highest point

County Seat: Honolulu

Island Flower: Ilima

Island Color: Yellow

OAHU—The Gathering Place

Beginnings

Oahu was created by three volcanoes. The first, called Kaena, formed about 5 million years ago. Two other volcanoes, Waianae and Koolau, developed on Kaena's sides. Over time, Kaena sank back beneath the ocean's surface, leaving Waianae and Koolau to shape the island. Koolau forms Oahu's east side, while Waianae makes up the west.

The Polynesians traveled to the Hawaiian Islands in outrigger canoes.

About 1,500 years ago, **Polynesians** began settling on Oahu and the other Hawaiian Islands. These people became the first Hawaiians. By 1795, a king named Kamehameha I had taken control of most of the Hawaiian Islands, including Oahu. Within 15 years, he conquered the rest of the archipelago, uniting the islands and their people under his rule.

By 1778, however, Europeans had also discovered Oahu. New animals and diseases were soon introduced to the island. This caused problems for the Hawaiian people and their environment.

Europeans quickly saw the potential in Oahu's south shore, setting up a small fishing village that later became Honolulu.

Speaking Hawaiian

The word *koolau*, pronounced "ko-oh-lau" means "facing the wind." The volcano and mountains were named because of their eastern, wind-facing position.

HAWAII

Oahu Timeline

500–800 AD
Polynesians sail across the Pacific Ocean and begin settling on the Hawaiian Islands.

1778
Captain James Cook becomes the first European to see Oahu.

1779
Captain Charles Clerke becomes the first European to set foot on Oahu.

1795
Kamehameha I claims the island of Oahu and becomes its king.

1893
The Hawaiian **monarchy** is overthrown by U.S. forces.

1941
Oahu's Pearl Harbor is attacked by Japan during World War II. The United States enters the war shortly after.

2024
Heavy rains in May cause flooding and landslides on the **windward** side of the island.

OAHU—The Gathering Place 7

People and Culture

The people of Oahu are known for their *aloha* spirit. They are warm and friendly to everyone. This welcoming spirit has been passed down from their **ancestors** and is part of who they are. Today's islanders work to keep it alive. They do this by sharing their **traditional** language, foods, music, and dances with others.

While Oahu is a place where people from different cultures live together, the island's best-known traditions come from the Polynesians who first settled there. Gatherings called *luaus* are held throughout the island. People come to eat traditional Hawaiian foods such as *lomi lomi* salmon and *haupia*, a coconut pudding. During the meal, entertainers play music, dance, and relate stories about Hawaiian history and **folklore**.

One of the best-known dishes served at luaus is kalua pork. This is pork that has been flavored with sea salt, wrapped in the leaves of a ti tree, and cooked in an underground oven.

Speaking Hawaiian

Aloha means "peace, love, compassion, and mutual respect." It is pronounced "a-LOH-a."

HAWAII

Floral garlands called *leis* are a common sight on Oahu. Leis represent the island's aloha spirit. They are given to welcome, congratulate, and honor locals and visitors alike. Making a lei involves a variety of techniques. These include weaving, braiding, and twisting. Each method gives a lei its own distinct look. Some of the most popular flowers seen in leis are orchids, plumerias, and carnations.

A lei maker typically uses a long sewing needle and a double strand of thread to string the flowers together.

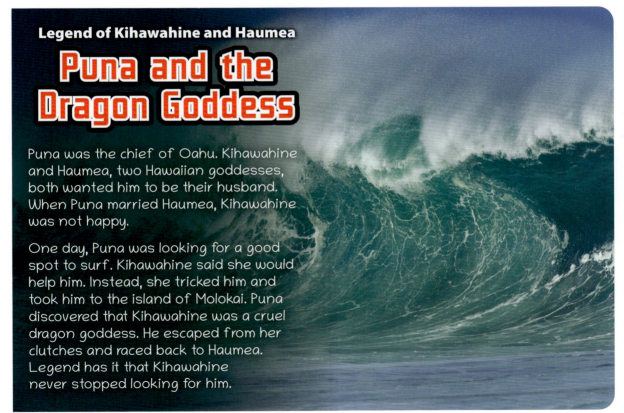

Legend of Kihawahine and Haumea

Puna and the Dragon Goddess

Puna was the chief of Oahu. Kihawahine and Haumea, two Hawaiian goddesses, both wanted him to be their husband. When Puna married Haumea, Kihawahine was not happy.

One day, Puna was looking for a good spot to surf. Kihawahine said she would help him. Instead, she tricked him and took him to the island of Molokai. Puna discovered that Kihawahine was a cruel dragon goddess. He escaped from her clutches and raced back to Haumea. Legend has it that Kihawahine never stopped looking for him.

OAHU—The Gathering Place

Exploring Oahu

Oahu has a mix of **urban** and **rural** sights to see. Honolulu offers shopping and entertainment on par with some of the world's largest cities. The countryside showcases the island's natural beauty, with rushing waterfalls, lush **rainforests**, and miles (km) of sandy beaches.

Honolulu

Honolulu serves as the gateway to the Hawaiian Islands. Most people traveling to Hawaii come through this city. It is also home to the state's largest shipping port, the University of Hawaii, and numerous museums and historic sites.

Lanai Lookout

The Lanai Lookout is found off the Kalanianaole Highway on Oahu's southeast shore. On a clear day, three other Hawaiian Islands—Lanai, Molokai, and Maui—can be viewed from here.

Hanauma Bay Nature Preserve

The Hanauma Bay Nature Preserve is home to a **coral reef** that is about 7,000 years old. More than 450 types of fish swim in its waters, along with marine animals such as dolphins and sea turtles.

Waimea Falls

One of Oahu's best-known waterfalls, Waimea Falls is found in the Koolau Mountains. It it is part of the Kamanui Stream. The waterfall has a drop of about 45 feet (14 m). Its waters eventually flow into the Pacific Ocean.

HAWAII

Diamond Head
Diamond Head is a mountain and **extinct** volcano. It rises to a height of 760 feet (232 m) above sea level. Believed to be about 300,000 years old, it was named a **National Natural Landmark** in 1968.

Lanikai Beach
Often referred to as Oahu's most beautiful beach, Lanikai extends for about 0.5 miles (0.8 km) along the island's east shore. The waters here are calm and crystal-blue, making it a picture-perfect spot to go swimming.

OAHU—The Gathering Place

Land and Climate

Waianae and Koolau, the two volcanoes that formed Oahu's land, were both shield volcanoes. A shield volcano looks like a big, pancake-shaped hill with gentle slopes on its sides. Over time, Waianae and Koolau were **eroded** by wind and rain. They now form the two mountain chains that run along the east and west sides of the island. The Koolau range stretches for 37 miles (60 km) along Oahu's eastern coast. The Waianae range runs along the west coast for about 22 miles (35 km). The highest point on the entire island is Mount Kaala. It is found in the Waianae range.

A wide valley called the Oahu Plain stretches between the two mountain chains. The area was used for agriculture in the past. Today, the valley is more developed. While it is still used for farming, small towns and commercial areas now dot the land.

Mount Kaala is Oahu's only peak to measure more than 4,000 feet (1,220 m) in height.

Speaking Hawaiian

Kaala means "fragrant mountain" in Hawaiian. It is pronounced "kā-ā'-la."

12 HAWAII

Oahu's climate is tropical. This means that the island is warm all year long. Oahu has two seasons, summer and winter. Summer temperatures range from about 73 to 86 degrees Fahrenheit (23 to 30 degrees Celsius), on average. In the winter, the weather is slightly cooler.

Most of Oahu's rain falls in the winter, with 2 to 3 inches (51 to 76 millimeters) each month. During the summer, less than 1 inch (25 mm) typically falls per month. However, there are exceptions to this pattern. In 1994, Oahu had one of the longest rainy periods ever recorded anywhere. From 1913 to 1916, it rained in Honomu Make every single day, for a total of 881 days in a row.

Average High Temperatures	
JAN	81°F (27°C)
FEB	81°F (27°C)
MAR	82°F (28°C)
APR	83°F (28°C)
MAY	85°F (29°C)
JUN	87°F (31°C)
JUL	88°F (31°C)
AUG	88°F (31°C)
SEP	88°F (31°C)
OCT	87°F (31°C)
NOV	84°F (29°C)
DEC	82°F (28°C)

Some Hawaiians enjoy the arrival of a storm as it produces higher waves, making the waters more active.

OAHU—The Gathering Place

Plants and Animals

ahu's land and surrounding waters are home to a variety of plants and animals. Some are unique to Oahu. Others can be found throughout the Hawaiian Islands or in other parts of the world.

Oahu Gardenia

The Oahu gardenia is found only in the Waianae and Koolau Mountains. This tree can grow about 50 feet (15 m) tall. Its flowers are white and fragrant. The Oahu gardenia is considered **endangered**, with fewer than 1,000 plants on the island.

Hawaiian Lionfish

The Hawaiian lionfish is **endemic** to the waters of the Hawaiian Islands, where it can be found at depths of up to 400 feet (120 m). This lionfish is easily recognized by its reddish-brown coloring and the spines on its **pectoral fins**. These spines are venomous and are normally used for defense.

14 HAWAII

Hawaiian Swimming Crab

The Hawaiian swimming crab is common throughout Hawaii. It can be found in waters up to 60 feet (18 m) deep. When fully grown, this crab's shell, or carapace, is about 3 inches (8 centimeters) across.

Oahu Tree Snail

Oahu is home to 19 types of tree snail. They live only in the forests of the Waianae and Koolau Mountains. There, they feed on **fungus** that grows on the leaves of native plants. These snails grow to be about 0.75 inches (2 cm) on average and are notable for their decorative shells.

Pohinahina

Pohinahina is native to most of Hawaii's main islands, where it grows close to the shoreline. A member of the mint family, its blooms are purple and form in clusters. Their fragrance is similar to that of the herb sage.

Hawaiian Coot

The Hawaiian coot can be seen on almost all of Hawaii's main islands, where it lives in coastal wetland areas. The coot has a varied diet, ranging from seeds and leaves to **crustaceans** and small fish. It will fly between islands to find food.

OAHU—The Gathering Place

Places to See

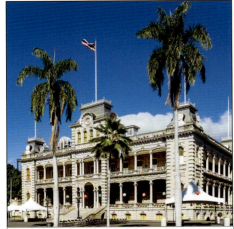

Oahu is home to the only royal palace in the United States. Built between 1879 and 1882, the Iolani Palace once served as the home of Hawaii's royal family. Today, it has been turned into a museum. Guests can walk down the Grand Hall and through the Throne Room, Music Room, State Dining Room, and others. The Iolani Palace also features beautiful grounds and a library with 14,000 rare books on Hawaiian culture.

The Iolani Palace opened to the public as a museum in 1978.

The Pearl Harbor National Memorial honors those who died at Pearl Harbor in the Japanese attack on December 7, 1941. The memorial's visitor center provides an overview of the attack through exhibits and videos. Visitors can then take a boat ride to the USS *Arizona* Memorial. The 184-foot (56-m) long memorial structure includes a shrine room. This houses a wall engraved with the names of the men killed on the USS *Arizona* that day.

The USS *Arizona* Memorial was built over the remains of the sunken battleship.

HAWAII

Hawaiian culture is on display at the Polynesian Cultural Center. This living museum is made up of villages that showcase traditional Polynesian life. Performers there demonstrate various arts and crafts, including dancing. The center also offers a luau, with live entertainment and a huge buffet of traditional Hawaiian foods.

The Polynesian Culture Center is consistently voted as Oahu's top tourist attraction. Close to 1 million people visit it every year.

Oahu's Waikiki Aquarium, which opened in 1904, is the second-oldest public aquarium in the United States. The aquarium focuses on marine life from the Pacific Ocean. More than 490 different **species** are on display there. These include tiger sharks and Hawaiian monk seals.

The Waikiki Aquarium is divided into 13 different exhibit areas, each with its own theme and associated sea life.

Oahu is the **most-visited** Hawaiian Island, with close to **6 million** guests per year.

In 2023, tourists spent more than **$9 billion** in Oahu alone.

Most of the tourists that visit Oahu are from the mainland United States, Canada, and Japan.

OAHU—The Gathering Place

Things to Do

Experienced surfers head to Ehukai Beach to take their chances on the Banzai Pipeline, one of the world's top surfing spots.

Hawaii is known as the place to go for surfing, and Oahu offers some of the best waves in the state. Serious surfers typically head to the island's north shore. There, they can test their skills on waves at Waimea Bay and Ehukai Beach. Less experienced surfers may want to head to Waikiki, on Oahu's south shore.

Oahu has plenty of trails for hikers. One of the best-known hikes is to the top of the Diamond Head crater. Hikers navigate three flights of stairs and at least one tunnel before reaching the summit. The Makapuu Point Lighthouse Trail leads to Oahu's southeasternmost point. Once there, hikers can walk around the lighthouse and look across the waters to the islands of Lanai and Molokai. In the winter, people can even watch humpback whales frolicking in the water.

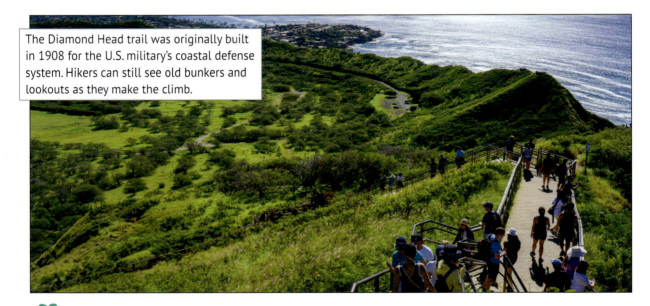

The Diamond Head trail was originally built in 1908 for the U.S. military's coastal defense system. Hikers can still see old bunkers and lookouts as they make the climb.

Speaking Hawaiian

Ehukai is the Hawaiian word for "sea spray." It is pronounced "eh-hoo-kai."

HAWAII

Horseback riding is a popular way for tourists to take in Oahu's natural environment. Riders can travel through a variety of scenic landscapes. There is even an opportunity to ride through the Kaaawa Valley. It is sometimes called "Jurassic" Valley because many scenes from the film *Jurassic Park* were filmed there.

The Kaaawa Valley provides riders with stunning scenery, ranging from towering cliffs to lush valleys.

For a more challenging nature experience, visitors to Oahu can go on a shark tour. Some of these offer people the opportunity to swim with sharks in Oahu's surrounding waters. Others feature cage dives. These tours send people underwater to see sharks up close from inside a protective cage. Sharks frequenting Oahu's waters include tiger, Galapagos, and sandbar sharks.

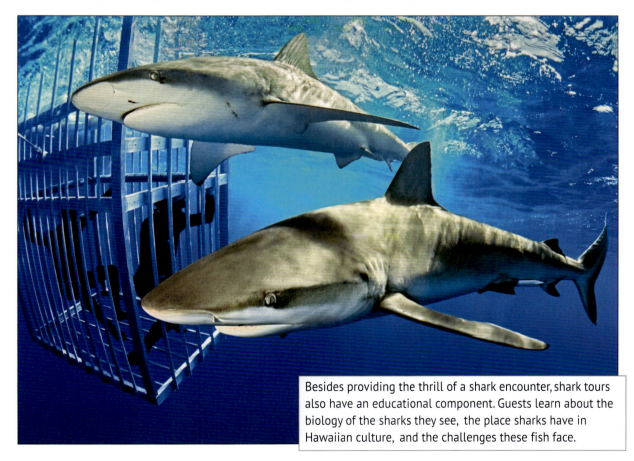

Besides providing the thrill of a shark encounter, shark tours also have an educational component. Guests learn about the biology of the sharks they see, the place sharks have in Hawaiian culture, and the challenges these fish face.

OAHU—The Gathering Place

Looking to the Future

Oahu's beaches are one of its main draws for tourists. Most people who come to the island will spend at least some time on a beach. However, some of Oahu's beaches are in danger of disappearing. **Climate change** is causing ocean levels to rise and more rain to fall. The beaches are gradually eroding as a result. Nowhere is this more obvious than in Waikiki, one of Oahu's main tourist spots. Waikiki's beaches are already narrowing as the ocean waters reach farther inland. During high tide, water is now coming up over the sidewalks. The many hotels in the area are in jeopardy of collapsing if water levels continue to rise.

Officials are looking at ways to delay or stop this damage. Waikiki's beaches have been replenished on occasion by bringing in sand from offshore. This may need to be done more often. There is also talk of building structures in the water that will help control the ocean waves.

Experts predict that, by 2050, Oahu could lose close to 40 percent of its beaches if steps are not taken to save them.

20 HAWAII

Over the past 20 years, the number of vehicles on Oahu's roads has doubled. This has led to increased traffic congestion throughout the island, especially in Honolulu.

SPOTLIGHT on CHANGE

A cap is just one way to control the effect tourists have on Oahu. What other measures could be put in place to maintain the island's tourism industry while still protecting its people, wildlife, and infrastructure?

As much as Oahu relies on the tourism industry, officials also acknowledge that tourists are causing problems for the island. Land is limited in Oahu, as it is on any island. As more tourists come to the island, its **infrastructure** becomes increasingly stressed. Oahu is known to have an issue with traffic **gridlock**. New building projects take land away from both people and wildlife.

Local officials are considering placing a cap on tourism. This means allowing only a certain number of people to visit Oahu at a given time. Some individual spots on the island have already moved forward with this idea, limiting the number of daily visitors to their site. By having more control over tourist traffic, they may be able to reduce the stress on Oahu's infrastructure, its people, and its natural environment.

OAHU—The Gathering Place

QUIZ YOURSELF ON Oahu

1 What percentage of Hawaii's population lives on Oahu?

2 When did Polynesians first start settling on Oahu?

3 What is the largest city in Oahu?

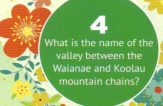
4 What is the name of the valley between the Waianae and Koolau mountain chains?

5 What is the name of the only royal residence in the United States?

6 How many people visit Oahu each year?

7 When did the Waikiki Aquarium open?

8 What is Kaaawa Valley sometimes called?

ANSWERS: 1. Approximately 75 percent **2.** About 1,500 years ago **3.** Honolulu **4.** Oahu Plain **5.** Iolani Palace **6.** Close to 6 million **7.** 1904 **8.** "Jurassic" Valley

22 HAWAII

Key Words

ancestors: people who were in someone's family in past times

archipelago: a group of islands

climate change: long-lasting changes to Earth's weather patterns

coral reef: a chain of coral found underwater

crustaceans: animals that have a hard outer shell and many legs, and typically live in water

endangered: at risk of no longer existing on Earth

endemic: native and restricted to a certain place

eroded: worn away

extinct: no longer active

folklore: the traditional stories and culture of a group of people

fungus: a plant-like organism

gridlock: a traffic jam affecting multiple streets

infrastructure: the basic facilities and systems serving a country, city, or area

monarchy: a form of government headed by a king or queen

National Natural Landmark: an area determined to be one of the best examples of biological or geological history in the United States

pectoral fins: fins situated just behind a fish's head

Polynesians: people who come from the islands of Polynesia

rainforests: dense forests that receive heavy annual rainfall and are made up of tall evergreen trees whose tops form a continuous layer

rural: relating to the countryside

species: a group of organisms that have similar features and can reproduce

traditional: based on information, beliefs, or customs handed down from one generation to another

urban: relating to the city

windward: facing the wind

Index

animals 6, 10, 14, 15, 17, 19

beaches 10, 11, 18, 20

Clerke, Captain Charles 7
Cook, Captain James 7

Diamond Head 11, 18

Hanauma Bay Nature Preserve 10, 11
hiking 18
Honolulu 5, 6, 10, 11, 21, 22
horseback riding 19

Iolani Palace 16, 22

Kaaawa Valley 19, 22
Kaena 6
Kamehameha I, King 6, 7
Koolau 6, 10, 12, 14, 15, 22

Lanai Lookout 10, 11
Lanikai Beach 11
leis 9
luaus 8, 17

Pacific Ocean 5, 7, 10, 11, 17
Pearl Harbor 7, 16
plants 14, 15
Polynesian Cultural Center 17
Polynesians 6, 7, 8, 17, 22

surfing 9, 18

tourism 5, 16, 17, 19, 20, 21, 22

Waianae 6, 12, 14, 15, 22
Waikiki 17, 18, 20, 22
Waimea Bay 18
Waimea Falls 10, 11

OAHU—The Gathering Place 23

Get the best of both worlds.

AV2 bridges the gap between print and digital.

The expandable resources toolbar enables quick access to content including **videos**, **audio**, **activities**, **weblinks**, **slideshows**, **quizzes**, and **key words**.

Animated videos make static images come alive.

Resource icons on each page help readers to further **explore key concepts**.

Published by Lightbox Learning Inc.
276 5th Avenue
Suite 704 #917
New York, NY 10001
Website: www.openlightbox.com

Copyright ©2026 Lightbox Learning Inc.
All rights reserved. No part of this publication may be reproduced, stored in a retrieval system, or transmitted in any form or by any means, electronic, mechanical, photocopying, recording, or otherwise, without the prior written permission of the publisher.

Library of Congress Cataloging-in-Publication Data

Names: Webster, Christine, author.
Title: Oahu "the gathering place" / Christine Webster.
Description: New York, NY : Lightbox Learning Inc., 2026. | Series: Hawaii | Includes index. | Audience: Grades 2-3
Identifiers: LCCN 2024047338 (print) | LCCN 2024047339 (ebook) | ISBN 9798874506681 (library binding) | ISBN 9798874506698 (paperback) | ISBN 9798874507527 (ebook other) | ISBN 9798874506704 (ebook other)
Subjects: LCSH: Oahu (Hawaii)--Juvenile literature. | Oahu (Hawaii)--Social life and customs--Juvenile literature.
Classification: LCC DU628.O3 W29 2026 (print) | LCC DU628.O3 (ebook) | DDC 996.9/3--dc23/eng/20241115
LC record available at https://lccn.loc.gov/2024047338
LC ebook record available at https://lccn.loc.gov/2024047339

Printed in Guangzhou, China
1 2 3 4 5 6 7 8 9 0 28 27 26 25 24

122024
101124

Project Coordinator: Heather Kissock
Designer: Terry Paulhus

Photo Credits
Every reasonable effort has been made to trace ownership and to obtain permission to reprint copyright material. The publisher would be pleased to have any errors or omissions brought to its attention so that they may be corrected in subsequent printings. The publisher acknowledges Getty Images, Alamy, Bridgeman Images, Shutterstock, and Wikimedia as its primary image suppliers for this title.

View new titles and product videos at www.openlightbox.com